ON GRIEF

Love, Loss, Memory

JENNIFER SENIOR

zando
NEW YORK

ON GRIEF by Jennifer Senior

Copyright © 2021 by The Atlantic Monthly Group

Photographs on pages 5, 9, 27, 51, 65 copyright © 2021 by Danna Singer
Photograph on page 59 copyright © 2021 by Jens Mortensen
Photograph on page 73 copyright © 2023 by Kelly McIlvaine

Zando
zandoprojects.com

First Edition: April 2023

Text and cover design by Oliver Munday

The publisher does not have control over and is not responsible
for author or other third-party websites (or their content).

Library of Congress Control Number: 2022946747

978-1-63893-074-7 (Paperback)
978-1-63893-075-4 (ebook)

10 9 8 7 6 5 4 3 2 1
Manufactured in the United States of America

Bobby McIlvaine's wallet (Danna Singer)

TWENTY YEARS GONE

September 2021

WHEN BOBBY MCILVAINE DIED ON September 11, 2001, his desk at home was a study in plate tectonics, coated in shifting piles of leather-bound diaries and yellow legal pads. He'd kept the diaries since he was a teenager, and they were filled with the usual diary things—longings, observations, frustrations—while the legal pads were marbled with more variety: aphoristic musings, quotes that spoke to him, stabs at fiction.

The yellow pads appeared to have the earnest beginnings of two different novels. But the diaries told a different kind of story. To the outside world, Bobby, 26, was a charmer, a striver, a furnace of ambition. But inside, the guy was a sage and a sap—philosophical about disappointments, melancholy when the weather changed, moony over girlfriends.

Less than a week after his death, Bobby's father had to contend with that pitiless still life of a desk. And so he began distributing the yellow legal pads, the perfect-bound diaries: to Bobby's friends; to Bobby's girlfriend, Jen, to whom he was about to propose. Maybe, he told them, there was material in there that they could use in their eulogies.

One object in that pile glowed with more meaning than all the others: Bobby's very last diary. Jen took one look and quickly realized that her name was all over it. Could she keep it?

Bobby's father didn't think. He simply said yes. It was a reflex that he almost instantly came to regret. "This was a decision we were supposed to make together," his wife, Helen, told him. Here was an opportunity to savor Bobby's company one last time, to hear his *voice*, likely saying something new. In that sense, the diary wasn't like a recovered photograph. It raised the prospect, however brief, of literary resurrection. How, Helen fumed, could her husband not want to know Bobby's final thoughts—ones he may have scribbled as recently as the evening of September 10? And how could he not share her impulse to take every last molecule of what was Bobby's and reconstruct him?

"One missing piece," she told me recently, "was like not having an arm."

Over and over, she asked Jen to see that final diary. Helen had plenty of chances to bring it up, because Jen lived with the McIlvaines for a time after September 11, unable to tolerate the emptiness of her own apartment. Helen was careful to explain that she didn't need the

A

object itself. All she asked was that Jen selectively photo-copy it.

Jen would say she'd consider it. Then nothing would happen. Helen began to plead. *I just want the words*, she'd say. *If Bobby's describing a tree, just give me the description of the tree.* Jen demurred.

The requests escalated, as did the rebuffs. They were having an argument now. Helen, Jen pointed out, already had Bobby's other belongings, other diaries, the legal pads.

When she finally left the McIlvaines' house for good, Jen slammed the door behind her, got into her car, and burst into tears. Shortly after, she wrote Helen a letter with her final answer: No, just no. If Helen wanted to discuss this matter any further, she'd have to do so in the presence of Jen's therapist.

Helen and her husband never saw Jen again. "She became a nonperson to me," Helen told me. Today, she can't so much as recall Jen's last name.

But for years, Helen thought about that diary. Her mind snagged on it like a nail; she needled her husband for giving it away; it became the subject of endless dis-cussion in her "limping group," as she calls it, a circle of six mothers in suburban Philadelphia who'd also lost children, though not on September 11. They became indignant on her behalf. A number proposed, only half jokingly, that they break into Jen's apartment and liberate the diary. "You don't get any more memories," one of the women told me. "So anything written, any video, any card—you cling to that. That's all you're going to get for life."

The McIlvaines would have to make do with what they already had. Eventually, they did. Three words of Bobby's became the family motto: *Life loves on*. No one could quite figure out which diary or legal pad it came from, but no matter. Helen wears a silver bracelet engraved with this phrase, and her husband got it tattooed in curlicue script on his upper arm.

HERE I SHOULD NOTE THAT I know and love the McIlvaine family. On my brother's first day of college, he was assigned to a seven-person suite, and because he arrived last, Bobby became his roommate. My brother often thinks about what a small miracle that was: If he'd arrived just 30 minutes earlier, the suite would have been an isomer of itself, with the kids all shuffled in an entirely different configuration. But thanks to a happy accident of timing, my brother got to spend his nights chattering away with this singular kid, an old soul with a snappity-popping mind.

Eight years later, almost to the day, a different accident of timing would take Bobby's life. He and my brother were still roommates, but this time in a two-bedroom apartment in Manhattan, trying to navigate young adulthood.

Back when Bobby was still alive, I would occasionally see the McIlvaines. They struck me as maybe the nicest people on the planet. Helen taught reading to kids who needed extra help with it, mainly in a trailer in the parking lot of a Catholic high school. Bob Sr. was a teacher who specialized in working with troubled adolescents; for a decade, he'd also owned a bar. Jeff, Bobby's younger brother, was just a kid in those days, but he was always unreasonably good-natured when he turned up.

And Bobby: My God. The boy was incandescent. When he smiled it looked for all the world like he'd swallowed the moon.

Then, on the morning of September 11, 2001, Bobby headed off to a conference at Windows on the World, a restaurant in a building to which he seldom had reason to go, for a media-relations job at Merrill Lynch he'd had only since July. My brother waited and waited. Bobby never came home. From that point forward, I watched as everyone in the blast radius of this horrible event tried to make sense of it, tried to cope.

Early on, the McIlvaines spoke to a therapist who warned them that each member of their family would grieve differently. *Imagine that you're all at the top of a mountain,* she told them, *but you all have broken bones, so you can't help each other. You each have to find your own way down.*

It was a helpful metaphor, one that may have saved the McIlvaines' marriage. But when I mentioned it to Roxane Cohen Silver, a psychology professor at UC Irvine who's spent a lifetime studying the effects of sudden, traumatic loss, she immediately spotted a problem with it: "That suggests everyone will *make it* down," she told me. "Some people never get down the mountain at all."

This is one of the many things you learn about mourning when examining it at close range: It's idiosyncratic, anarchic, polychrome. A lot of the theories you read about grief are great, beautiful even, but they have a way of erasing individual experiences. Every mourner has a very different story to tell.

That therapist was certainly right, however, in the most crucial sense: After September 11, those who had been close to Bobby all spun off in very different directions. Helen stifled her grief, avoiding the same supermarket she'd shopped in for years so that no one would ask how she was. Jeff, Bobby's lone sibling, had to force his way through the perdition of survivor's guilt. Bob Sr. treated his son's death as if it were an unsolved

A

murder, a cover-up to be exposed. Something was fishy about 9/11.

And then there was Jen. She's married now, has two terrific kids, but she wonders sometimes, when she's quarreling with her husband or feeling exasperated with her life, what it would have been like if she'd been with Bobby all this time. I tracked her down in April, and of course she's nothing like the heartless villainess I had come to imagine her to be. That was just the story I'd told myself, the one I'd used to make sense of the senseless, to give shape to my own rage. Like I said: We all need our stories.

One thing I knew when I finally visited her, though: I wanted to see that diary. And I wanted the McIlvaines to see it too. "I'm not a saver," she said when we first met up for cocktails. My heart froze.

But she still had it, just so you know.

*Bobby McIlvaine, with his parents, Helen and Bob Sr., at his
Princeton graduation in 1997. Bobby's body was found in the
wreckage of the Twin Towers. (Danna Singer; original photo by
Charles F. Wennogle Sr. courtesy of the McIlvaine family)*

———

TELL ME ABOUT YOUR SON.

Helen welcomed this invitation the first time she heard it, because it focused her thinking, gave her an outlet for her grief. But soon it filled her with dread, and she felt herself straining under the weight of it. How can you possibly convey who your firstborn was or what he meant to you?

Helen usually starts by telling people that Bobby went to Princeton, but that's hardly because she's status fixated. It's because she and Bob Sr. did not expect to have a child who went to an Ivy League school. They both went to state schools in Pennsylvania, not even particularly well-known ones. Both of their kids were sporty. But when Bobby was eight, his third-grade teacher said to them—and they both remember her exact words—"Start saving your pennies." This one's education might cost you.

"The amount of things that had to go right for my brother to go to Princeton were, like, astronomical," says Jeff, a high-school biology teacher and track coach in Somerdale, New Jersey. "To us, it was like someone from our family becoming the president."

This is how everyone in the family remembers Bobby: as a sui generis creature, exceptional and otherworldly, descended from the heavens through a basketball hoop.

He was an intense student. He was an even more intense athlete, competitive to the point of insolence. Writing in *The Philadelphia Inquirer* last year, Mike Sielski, an old high school classmate of Bobby's, described him as "all bones and acute angles and stiletto elbows" on the basketball court. It was a goose-pimpling story, one he had occasion to write because another classmate of theirs had unearthed 36 seconds of video from 1992, in which a teenage Bobby McIlvaine throws an immaculate pass that sets up an immaculate shot that flies right over the teenage head of . . .

Kobe Bryant.

Bobby scored 16 points off Kobe and his team that day, in addition to setting up that floater.

When he arrived at college, Bobby retained a bit of that alpha-dog streak. He was still competitive, even while playing mindless, made-up dorm games. He wasn't bashful about ribbing friends. He was tall and handsome and had a high level of confidence in his sense of style, which may or may not have been justified. "There were times you wanted him to step back and not be so serious and intense," says Andre Parris, a former suitemate and one of Bobby's closest friends. "But it was part of who and what he was, and what he thought he had to do to get ahead."

A

What "getting ahead" meant to Bobby was complicated. Financial worries are all over his journals from those years (*I don't feel like a real person sitting here with no money*, reads one typical entry). Yet he was conflicted about what it might take to make money, flummoxed by all the kids who were beating a dutiful path to business school. (*Is youth really just a hobby?* he asked about them, with evident pique.) He wanted to be a writer. Which paid nothing, obviously.

This conflict continued into his brief adulthood. He spent two years in book publishing before realizing that it was no way to make a living, and switched instead to corporate PR. He could still write his novels on the side.

But for all Bobby's hunger and swagger, what he mainly exuded, even during his college years, was warmth, decency, a corkscrew quirkiness. He doted on girlfriends. He gave careful advice. His senior year, he took a modern-dance class because, well, why not? It would be fun. And different. His final project involved physically spelling out his girlfriend's name.

That was just a lark, though. Bobby's real intellectual passion was African American culture and history. After Bobby died, the McIlvaines got not one but two condolence notes from Toni Morrison, with whom he'd taken a class. The second came with the term paper he'd written for her. "It is certainly one of the more accomplished and insightful," she wrote, "as was he." His senior thesis received an honorable mention for the main prize in the department of African American studies.

At his funeral, Bobby's oldest friends spoke of what a role model he was to them. I was five years older than Bobby, which meant I mainly saw him as charming and adorable, intelligent and unstoppable.

But strangely, I wanted to impress him too. When I started my job at *New York* magazine, writing short features in the theater section each week, Bobby gave me grief about ending each one of them with a quote. At first I was annoyed, defensive—*the little shit*—but in hindsight, it's amazing that I cared so much about this 22-year-old's opinion, and even more amazing that he'd read me attentively enough to discover an incipient tic. To this day, I credit Bobby with teaching me a valuable lesson: If you're going to cede the power of the last word to someone else, you'd better be damn sure that person deserves it.

BOB MCILVAINE SR. cries easily and regularly when you speak to him. Everyone in the family knows this and has grown accustomed to it—his grief lives close to the surface, heaving up occasionally for air. He cried at our

A

first lunch after the McIlvaines picked me up at the train station a few months ago; he cried again just minutes into our first chat when the two of us were alone; he cried in a recent interview with Spike Lee for a documentary series about 9/11 on HBO.

In talking with Bob Sr., something heartbreaking and rudely basic dawned on me: September 11 may be one of the most-documented calamities in history, but for all the spools of disaster footage we've watched, we still know practically nothing about the last moments of the individual dead. It's strange, when you think about it, that an event so public could still be such a punishing mystery. Yet it is, and it is awful—the living are left to perseverate, to let their imaginations run amok in their midnight corrals.

For Bob Sr., what that meant was wondering where Bobby was and what he was doing when the chaos began. For years, that was all he could think about. The idea of Bobby suffering tortured him. Was he incinerated? Was he asphyxiated? Or even worse? "I think Bobby jumped," he shouted up the stairs one day to his wife. The thought nearly drove Helen mad.

Over time, it became clear that Bobby didn't jump. Bobby's was one of fewer than 100 civilian corpses recovered from the wreckage. But it haunted Bob Sr. that he never saw the body. At the morgue on September 13, the pathologist strongly advised him against viewing it. Only years later—four? five? he can no longer remember—did he finally screw up the courage to go to the medical examiner's office in New York City and get the official report.

That's when everything changed. "My whole thesis—everything I jump into now—is based upon his injuries," he tells me. "Looking at the body, I came to the conclusion that he was walking in and bombs went off."

A controlled demolition, he means. That is how he thinks Bobby died that day, and how the towers eventually fell: from a controlled demolition. It was an inside job, planned by the U.S. government, not to justify the war in Iraq—that was a bonus—but really, ultimately, to destroy the 23rd floor, because that's where the FBI was investigating the use of gold that the United States had unlawfully requisitioned from the Japanese during World War II, which it then leveraged to bankrupt the Soviet Union. The planes were merely for show.

DOES A MAN WAKE UP on September 12, 2001, and believe such a thing? No. This belief takes shape over the span of years, many years.

That first year, Bob Sr. was numb. His sole objective was to get through each day. But he eventually got

A

involved in a group called 9/11 Families for Peaceful Tomorrows, protesting the wars in Afghanistan and Iraq. "It opened up my life," he tells me. "I became very active. That's how I grieved. It was perfect."

Before Bobby went to Princeton, Bob Sr. had been indifferent to politics, voting sometimes for Democrats and sometimes for Republicans—including, he thinks, Ronald Reagan. "I was not a well-read person," he says. "I owned a bar in the city. If I even mentioned the word *progressive*, my customers probably would have shot me."

But then Bobby started taking classes with Princeton's glamorous tenured radicals. He started writing for the school's *Progressive Review*. His father devoured everything he wrote. Soon, he had Bob Sr. reading Howard Zinn's *A People's History of the United States* and *Z Magazine*, the radical monthly. Bob Sr. has been interested in politics ever since. "That's all because of Bobby."

So this anti-war activity? It *was* perfect—a natural outlet for him.

But as time wore on, Bob Sr. got impatient. In 2004, he went down to Washington to hear Condoleezza Rice speak to the 9/11 Commission, and her testimony—or lack thereof, he'd say—so enraged him that he left in a huff, cursing in the halls of Congress. "I wanted answers," he explains. Yet no answers were forthcoming. That's when he realized: The government was hiding something. "I became militant," he says. "To this day, I'm very militant."

Bob Sr. is a bespectacled, soft-spoken man, slender and slightly stooped. But his affect is deceptive. We're sitting in the upstairs den of the McIlvaines' three-bedroom home in Oreland, Pennsylvania, the same house where Bobby and Jeff grew up. It's sweet, modest, cluttered with family pictures. But this room has been transformed into a 9/11 research bunker, stuffed with books and carefully organized files—by event, subject, country. The largest piece of art on the wall is a world map freckled with pins marking every country that's invited Bob Sr. to tell his story.

"I speak out so much, the word just spreads," he tells me. "I'll show you Italy." Pictures and clippings from a Rome film festival, he means, because he appeared in the documentary *Zero: Inchiesta sull'11 settembre*. He got to walk the red carpet. "The Russians came over. They spent two days here, wanted to hear what I had to say." Meaning Russian state news agencies. They parked themselves on the McIlvaines' back deck. "France came here, stayed a few days to talk." Same deal, though he doesn't remember which media outfit. ("My dad is practically a celebrity in that community," Jeff told me.)

Crucial to Bob Sr.'s understanding of September 11—that it was the cynical skulduggery of the U.S. government, not a grisly act of terrorism by jihadists using commercial planes filled with helpless civilians—is the work of Architects & Engineers for 9/11 Truth, which popularized the idea that jet fuel couldn't burn at a high enough temperature to melt beams into molten steel. This is, it should go without saying, contrary to all observable fact.

But this theory is what Bob Sr. is eager to illustrate for me. He has visuals prepared, lots of building diagrams. I tell him we'll get there; I just want to ask a few more questions about those early days—

He's disappointed. "Everything I've done in my life is based upon those seconds." This is something he very much wants to discuss.

And so we discuss it. Only a preplanned detonation, he argues, could bring down those towers, and only a lobby embroidered with explosives could explain the injuries to Bobby's body. He has the full medical examiner's report.

It is very upsetting to read. Most of Bobby's head—that beautiful face—was missing, as was most of his right arm. The details are rendered in generic diagrams and the dispassionate language of pathology ("Absent: R upper extremity, most of head"), as well as a chilling pair of responses on a standard checklist.

Hair color: None.

Eye color: None.

But a subtle thing made Bob Sr. think something was amiss. The report describes many lacerations and fractures, but they appear almost entirely on the front of Bobby's body. The back of his corpse is basically described as pristine, besides multiple fractures to what remained of his head.

The story we've told ourselves all these years is that Bobby had already left the building when the planes hit. Bobby didn't work in the World Trade Center; from what we could piece together, he'd gone to Windows on the World simply to help a new colleague set up for a morning presentation at an all-day conference, not to attend it. So Bobby did his part, was our assumption, then said his goodbyes and was making his way back to nearby Merrill Lynch when he was suddenly killed in the street by flying debris.

Bob Sr. doesn't buy it. If that were true—if Bobby were moving *away* from the World Trade Center— wouldn't he have fallen forward? Wouldn't there be injuries on his *back*? "If you're running away, it'd be

A

more of a crushing type of thing," he tells me. "Probably every bone in his body would be breaking."

I tell him I'm not a pathologist, but it seems just as plausible to me that he heard the roaring sound of a plane flying too low and too fast, or maybe the sound of a hijacked aircraft hitting the North Tower itself, and turned around to see what had happened and never knew what hit him.

He rejects this explanation. "My theory is he was walking *into* the building at the time, because he had the conference up there."

"I thought his conference started at 8:30?" I ask. The first plane hit at 8:46 a.m. That would have meant Bobby was arriving late.

"I thought it started at 9," Bob Sr. says.

"Isn't there a way to find out?" I ask.

"You know, to tell you the truth, I never . . ."

He'd never checked.

BREAKFAST AND REGISTRATION for the conference began at 8 o'clock. Opening remarks were scheduled for 8:30. Bobby's colleague was scheduled to speak at 8:40. The full brochure is available on the 9/11 Memorial & Museum's website.

When I eventually visit Jen—she of the purloined diary, the woman to whom Bobby was about to be engaged—she shows me the daily planner that was sitting on his desk at Merrill. It's cluttered with appointments. But the day of September 11 is blank. Whatever he was doing was not significant enough to merit its own entry.

My brother also tells me that he still has the note Bob Sr. left for him on his kitchen table on Thursday, September 13. It said that an investigator with the New York City Police Department, Joe Gagliardi, had just come by to drop off the wallet they'd pulled from Bobby's pocket. One line in particular stood out. *He was found on the perimeter.* Not near the lobby.

"Was he really?" Bob Sr. says when I phone him and ask him about the note. He'd completely forgotten that he'd written it. "If that's true, that's great." He thinks for a moment. "Though the perimeter—he still could have been 10 feet away. He certainly wasn't 100 feet from the building."

I then tell him about the conference schedule, which actually did leave open the possibility that he was 100 feet from the building. If he'd left before his colleague started speaking—or the opening remarks—he could have been quite close to his office at Merrill Lynch, a five-minute walk away. Bob Sr. takes it all in. He repeats that he finds Bobby's injuries too extreme, too savage,

A

to be caused by flying debris. "But you know what?" he finally says. "That's no longer relevant to me. My whole thing is who did it and why. It's been 20 years and I *still* can't get any answers."

IT TAKES ME SOME TIME, but eventually I summon the courage to ask Bob Sr. an obvious question: What makes his claims about the destruction of the World Trade Center more credible than the claims of, for instance, Donald Trump supporters who say the 2020 election was stolen?

"I can believe it was stolen!" he tells me. "But I'm not going to go around preaching that, because *I don't know.* Because I'm doing *my* homework." Bob Sr. is always reading. His latest is a biography of Allen Dulles. "Probably 99.9 percent of the people that you will find in those radical groups—the Oath Keepers, whatever— they really haven't done any research."

But then he adds that he sympathizes with Trump voters, as much as he despises Trump himself. "This country hasn't done anything for them in such a long time. So you can't blame them for voting for him."

BOB SR. ASKS IF I WOULD like to see Bobby's wallet. I didn't realize he had it, but he does, stuffed in a biohazard bag, itself entombed in a plastic box in the room that once belonged to Bobby. He carefully opens them for me.

"Helen and Jeff have never seen this," he tells me.

They haven't?

"No."

The wallet is covered in dust, still, and faintly redolent of that World Trade Center tang, a scent once so powerful that New Yorkers could smell it in their eyes. He starts pulling out a 26-year-old's modest possessions: a Pennsylvania driver's license, a Visa card, some kind of work or building ID, a library card. The wallet still contains $13 in cash, but the money is disintegrating, almost completely rotted away.

"The only thing I do is 9/11 stuff," Bob Sr. says. "My whole basis of everything revolves around the day."

This is not, it should be said, anything like what Helen does with her days. A two-decade investigation into 9/11 was not part of her retirement plan. In one of our earliest conversations, she specifically told me that she'd walk across the United States to *not* discover some of the things that Bob Sr. has learned. So as he and I sit here, inspecting a wallet that she's never seen, I ask: Doesn't all this searching, this interrogating, have unhealthy consequences for his marriage?

A

He readily admits that it does: "We'd socialize and she'd catch me saying stuff, and she would go nuts. She'd say, 'Do not talk about 9/11.' But then someone would come up to me and say, 'Can I ask you about it?' And I'd start talking. Then she'd find out about it. She'd get so upset." They now tend to socialize separately. "I will talk 9/11 with anyone I see, if they want to talk about it," he says. "And I think that's why I don't have many friends. They're *afraid* I'm going to talk about it."

It may be hard to imagine why anyone would want to spend so much time immersed in the story, sensations, and forensics of his son's death. But for Bob Sr., that's precisely the point: to keep the grief close. "I don't want to get away from it," he tells me. He *wants* to stay at the top of the mountain. This is how he spends time in Bobby's company—by solving this crime, by exposing the truth about the abuses of American empire. "Doing what I'm doing, that's really helped me, because I think of him every day. Every time I talk, I talk about Bobby."

He's aware that there are other ways to spend time with Bobby that wouldn't be quite so excruciating. He could read his diaries, for example. To this day, he feels terrible that he handed that last one off to Jen. He felt so guilty about it for so long that he was still mentioning it in interviews in 2011. A British newspaper referred to it as "the journal episode."

"I'm just not that big on the journals," he tells me. "They don't mean that much to me."

So what means the most to you? I ask.

"That he was murdered," he says.

A

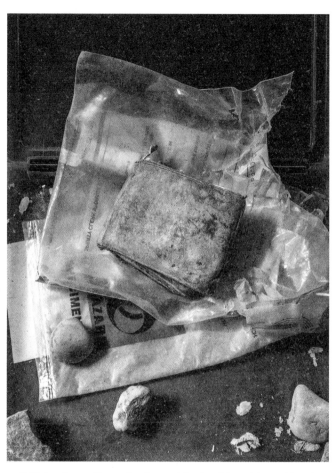

Bobby's wallet is still covered in dust, and faintly redolent of the World Trade Center tang that hung over New York in the fall of 2001. (Danna Singer)

ON THE MORNING OF September 11, Helen, the most stoic of the McIlvaines, was the only one who panicked. Jeff knew that his brother didn't work in the World Trade Center. Bob Sr., who was teaching that day in the adolescent psych unit of a local hospital, treated the macabre, smoldering towers like a news event and, along with everyone else, began watching the coverage on TV.

Helen, however, took one look at the television and needed to sit down. She knew it seemed ridiculous, superstitious, but she'd spoken with Bobby the night before and forgotten to end the conversation the way she always did: "Be careful." She'd later say those words to his casket as it was lowered into his grave.

By midday, when no one had heard from Bobby, everyone in the family felt like Helen. Yes, the cell towers were down in Lower Manhattan and the phones were working only sporadically, but surely Bobby, who could spend hours on the phone talking with his parents (*How do you guys find so much to talk about?* his friends always asked), would have found a way to call, and Jen had heard nothing, which *really* made no sense. Bobby had just asked her father for permission to marry her two days earlier.

In the late afternoon, Andre, his close friend and old suitemate, finally reached a woman at Merrill Lynch who awkwardly told him that Bobby and a colleague had been scheduled to attend a conference at Windows on the World that morning and no one had heard from them since. Andre called the McIlvaines.

"That first night was probably worse than after we found out for sure that he'd died," Jeff says, "because we had no idea what had happened. I couldn't get that out of my head—that he was *in* that, you know?"

They slept in the den, the three of them. Jen stayed in her own living room that night, glued to the TV.

On Wednesday morning, Jeff and Bob Sr. were too agitated to remain in Oreland. They took a train to New York and made a fruitless tour of the city's triage centers. Nothing. My brother stood on line at a missing-persons center; Andre ran a command center out of his apartment, working the phones and every lead he had; Jeff checked every website he could find. *Refresh, refresh, refresh.*

Jen sat and waited.

Bob Sr. spent Wednesday night in my brother and Bobby's apartment, sleeping in his son's bed.

The next day, Andre got a call from the NYPD, this time with grim news: Everyone needed to go immediately to the armory on Lexington Avenue.

Once again, Andre had to tell the McIlvaines. Helen calmly did as she was told—grateful, at least, to at last have something specific to do.

The armory was a seething mass of the desperate. Hundreds of families were lined up outside, carrying posters with faces of their loved ones. A minister escorted my brother, Jen, Andre, and the McIlvaine family inside. Helen gave him Bobby's name. A police officer approached her from across the room. "Are you the mother?"

Much of what followed was a blur. They were shown to a private room where grief counselors descended on them. Then something unusual happened: Rudy Giuliani walked in.

The mayor was unaccompanied. Without aides, without cameras, nothing. He looked genuinely relieved to have a family to console at that moment, with so many bereaved New Yorkers still twisting in limbo, posting flyers with pictures of the missing on lamp-posts, chain-link fences, hospital walls.

Giuliani embraced everyone. Then he took a seat opposite the McIlvaines. He uttered just five words: "Tell me about your son."

IF BOB SR. CHOSE TO feed his grief, Helen chose to starve hers. She spoke about it with her limping group, because they understood. But she was determined not to be, as she puts it, "At-Least-I'm-Not-Helen." Living with the impossible was hard enough. But to be in the position of having to console others about her misfortune, or to manage their discomfort, or, worst of all, to smile politely through their pity—that was more than she could bear. Helen can still rattle off a list of all the well-meaning things people said that stung.

No parent should bury a child.

You will never be the same.

I was with my children last night and realized you'll never have something like that again.

Did people not realize that they were building a moat, not a bridge, when they said such things? That they were drawing attention to the pretty castles they lived in, their walls still lined with luck?

That first year was brutal. Once, while she was sitting in a diner with some friends, one of them started going on and on about the musical talents of her son. "I wanted to scream," Helen says. "I had to get out. I couldn't listen to somebody else talk about their child. For years. I couldn't."

The second year wasn't much better. She tried going to Italy on a tour with a friend. She says she came across as cold, distant, strange. She dreaded the most innocuous question: *Have any kids?*

A

Work helped. Her students needed her, and her colleagues were great. "Except I didn't want their help, because it was too soon," Helen says. "So afterwards, a few years down the road, I looked like I'd healed. And it wasn't true. I *wanted* to talk about it sometimes. But I had to find other means to do it, because I'd kind of shut that door."

I can't decide whether this corresponds with the Helen I've come to know. Maybe?

Helen: She wears little or no makeup. She is exceedingly good-humored. She is always brimming with questions about your life. She's the kind of person who goes along with any plan and can spend 20 minutes in a drugstore trying on funny pairs of reading glasses with you.

We actually did this together in Florida a couple of years ago. We both happened to be visiting my mom.

So the reserve she's describing is a little foreign to me. "I have a weird personality," she tells me. "I can cry over a blouse that I ruined in the laundry and then be stoic for something . . ." She trails off, but I believe the word she's looking for is *big*.

But with Bobby . . . ! Bobby brought out her more emotional self, because he was such a sensitive kid. "Once, after about half an hour of listening to his woe-is-me girlfriend stories," she tells me, "I said to him,

'You do understand I've been married to Dad for almost 30 years and I've never given him this much thought, right?'" But of course she loved every minute of it.

The last time she saw Bobby was two nights before he died. Not an hour before, he had asked Jen's father for permission to marry her; now the two families were having dinner at a restaurant in Lambertville, New Jersey, where Jen had an apartment. Helen took one look at her son and saw that his forehead was still shimmering with sweat. She reached under the table to find his hand. He locked his pinkie with hers. They stayed that way until the food came.

AROUND THE TENTH ANNIVERSARY of September 11, Helen realized that she was not all right. She'd lost a child, so maybe this was what her new life was destined to be: not all right. But she wasn't convinced. Somewhere along the way, her toughness, her steadfast refusal to be a victim—it had backfired. "I found myself being petty. And bickering. I found myself being too gossipy sometimes."

I've never heard Helen say a cross word about anyone. Even when I mention that I'll soon be seeing Jen, she reacts with anxiety, not bitterness. She doesn't want to open old wounds. They were both suffering terribly back then; neither was her finest self.

Okay, but what if she lends me the diary? I ask.

"Oh my God. Would you marry me?"

But this is today's Helen. The Helen of a decade ago decided she wasn't who she wanted to be. Her therapy had stalled. She had trouble managing her anger. "My life just feels so amazingly off kilter," she wrote in a reminiscence marking the tenth anniversary.

She'd kept too much in, and she was fermenting in her own brine.

Not long after, she started seeing a different therapist. This one was spiritual. That new perspective changed everything. "She really believes that we don't see all."

Even before Bobby died, Helen was a big fan of self-help books. But after September 11, she bought them by the dozen, hoovering up everything she could about loss. She found Elisabeth Kübler-Ross indispensable— not so much for her writing about the five stages of grief, though that was fine, but for her writing about life after death.

Kübler-Ross once considered a belief in the afterlife a form of denial. But starting in the mid-1970s, she had a change of heart, compiling thousands of testimonies from those who'd had near-death experiences in order to show that our souls outlast us.

"I looked at life-after-death books, but they were too faith-based," Helen says. "I *wanted* to believe what I was taught in my Catholic upbringing. But what I liked about Kübler-Ross is that she had a science background."

It was precisely because she was a scientist, of course, that Kübler-Ross's fellow physicians were so dismayed by this strange turn in her interests. They thought it kooky and unrigorous, a stain on her legacy. I tell this to Helen. She laughs. "Bet they didn't sell millions of books."

Kübler-Ross used a hokey but intuitive metaphor to describe the body and soul: Our bodies are our mortal coils, our "cocoons"; when we die, we shudder them off and our souls—our "butterflies"—are released into the wilds of the universe. Helen cherished this idea. It was a notion that could redeem a violently, capriciously abbreviated life. "One day I actually thought, *What if there's a hierarchy and Bobby's a part of that, and he just came down as a human for a bit?*"

She and Bob Sr. began watching *Supernatural* and *Buffy the Vampire Slayer*, shows they'd never have imagined watching before.

And here in this world, Helen came to understand that there was nothing to be gained by bottling up her grief. At age 60, she took up running, not only because it felt good but because it allowed her to cry. She started expressing herself more. She noticed one day that the tempest of grievances she unloosed in her therapist's office were all so trivial, so petty, so *pointless*. What was she getting so worked up about?

Now she's doing the very thing the self-help books tell you to do: letting stuff go. She tells me about a friend whose towering self-involvement used to infuriate her. But recently, she chatted with her on the phone and decided just to enjoy the good bits.

Wow, I say. What makes you so forgiving?

"It wasn't serving me well."

YOU KNOW WHAT RADICAL acceptance is? Living with a husband who has dedicated his life to spreading the word that the United States deliberately orchestrated the collapse of the World Trade Center and then conspired to cover it up. Forget all the chipper advice columns about how to get along with your Trump-loving uncle at Thanksgiving. How do you get on in your decades-long marriage after your son has died and your spouse wakes up each morning livid as an open wound and determined to expose the truth?

Helen would be lying if she said this didn't cause friction.

"There were many moments where I was like, *Oh, please*," she says. She was perfectly open to some of the things Bob Sr. said. "But a lot of it was emotional, and a lot of it, I couldn't trace to find out myself, and I'm not a go-on-a-website kind of person. I didn't want to burst his bubble by constantly saying, 'Well, did you check, is it a valid website?'"

Perhaps the more challenging issue, the nuts-and-bolts-of-living-in-a-marriage issue, was daily conversation. Bob Sr.'s single-minded focus meant that any conversation could segue without warning into September 11. She'd come downstairs and tell him she was thinking about buying a new sweater; he'd reply by asking if she knew that the government had lied about the actual date of Osama bin Laden's death.

"So has it gotten in the way?" she asks. "Yeah, many times. We'd be going somewhere, and I'd say to Bob, 'You *cannot* talk about 9/11.' And he'd say, 'Well, they ask me about it.' I fell for that for the first 99 times until my therapist said, 'That's not good enough.' When we're out at a social event, we're out. I don't want to be always *victim, victim, victim*."

How do you handle it now, I ask, if you feel another soliloquy coming on?

"Now I say, 'Bob, you have the I-won't-talk-about-anything-else-but-9/11 look on your face.' We've come to a point where we can actually joke about it."

Helen wants me to understand: There are some aspects of Bob Sr.'s obsessions that she doesn't merely

A

tolerate; she actively supports them. Two years ago, she listened to a presentation by Architects & Engineers for 9/11 Truth and found it persuasive. It's the other parts of his narrative, which keep evolving, that leave her at loose ends. "If I were him, I'd just stick with the buildings," she says. I ask if she's up-to-date on his latest theory, involving Japanese gold. She shakes her head. "I don't even hear it," she says. "I'm defending the person, not the view."

Long ago, Helen realized that "9/11 truth," as Bob Sr. likes to call it, had sunk its hooks into her husband, and she's never thought it her place to pry them loose. "I'm very protective of him," she says. "If he decided to be a male stripper in an old people's home, it's okay with me. He has to be who he has to be, because damn it, this happened, you know? And if that's going to give him comfort—"

She interrupts herself, gives an embarrassed smile. "Get that visualization out of your head."

Helen would never dream of abandoning this dear man. He was Bobby's Little League coach. The one who organized races around the house when the kids were little, using a piece of tape for the finish line. Bob Sr. was her only suitor who ever suggested they play sports together—the others thought that was strictly for the fellas.

And now he's the only other person in the world who understands what it feels like to have raised Bobby McIlvaine and lost him.

She walks me over to the wall with a giant framed poster she had custom-made for her husband five years ago. It's a periodic table of Bob Sr., basically—dozens of images of him, all tidily laid out in a grid. Bob Sr. talking to Rosie O'Donnell. Bob Sr. giving an interview on French television. Bob Sr. speaking at a forum about the 9/11 Commission report, captured on C-SPAN. "I gave him that on his 70th birthday," she says. She went online, punched his name into Google, and voilà. A hero's gallery. "I love looking at it." He's become the superstar, strangely, that his son never had the chance to be.

Bob Sr.'s crusade may look to the outside world like madness. Helen sees it as an act of love. "He's almost going to war for his son," she tells me. "He's being a father in the best way he knows how. How can I not allow that?"

MOST THEORIES OF GRIEF, particularly the ones involving stages, are more literary than literal. People don't mourn sequentially, and they certainly don't mourn logically. But there's an aspect of one of those models I keep circling back to whenever I think of the McIlvaines. It's

A

the "yearning and searching" stage of grief, first described by the British psychiatrists Colin Murray Parkes and John Bowlby in the 1960s. "When searching," Parkes writes, "the bereaved person feels and acts as if the lost person were recoverable, although he knows intellectually that this is not so."

How Bob Sr. searches is obvious. But it occurs to me, after speaking with Helen, that perhaps her years-long preoccupation with Bobby's final diary is her equivalent of Bob Sr.'s obsessions. "Yes!" she says when I tentatively raise the possibility. "Yes, yes. It's 'If I can't have *this*, then I'll have *that*.'"

Yet here's what's curious. Helen has two earlier diaries of Bobby's. She also has stacks of legal pads of his writing, many with diarylike entries in them. But she's barely dipped into them at all.

One reason is practical: They're hard to decipher. Bobby's handwriting is neat but small and slightly peculiar. Another is instinctive: For a long time, Helen feared that reading them would be a violation of a sacred boundary, "like going into his room without knocking." Yet another is how much pain it causes her. "I tried today again," she wrote in another reminiscence on the tenth anniversary of Bobby's death. "I thought, 'If I don't tackle these before I'm dead, who will?'" She lasted 10 minutes. Bob Sr. has never looked at them at all.

"But somewhere I did find the words *Life loves on*," Helen tells me.

I've been meaning to ask her about this, because I'm now reading Bobby's diaries and legal pads, and I can't find the phrase anywhere. Does she still not know where it came from?

She doesn't. She thought he'd written it about a close family friend who'd died, but she was wrong. I tell her I'll keep looking.

I take one of the two diaries back to my hotel that night. And I realize, as I'm reading, that there's probably another reason Helen never dug too deep into either one of them. They're from his freshman and sophomore years of college, when he was still a proto-person, still essentially a kid. He was clearly older when he scribbled in some of those legal pads, but they're chaotic and undated. Only the diaries feel manageable and chronological, and they read like the musings of a boy in his late teens—florid, soulful, a little mushy. He doesn't sound at all like the Bobby of September 11, 2001, who was almost 27 years old.

Yet I still get a kick out of them, and those chaotic legal pads, especially the parts about writing. Even at 19, Bobby was trying to find his voice, sometimes shifting from the first person to the third to see if he liked it better (and then saying so in the margins—*third-person*

A

experiment!). They're filled with exhortations and reminders to himself: *I need to stay true to my voice, whatever it is. I write horrible stuff in other people's voices.* And my favorite: *Hope is even more important than talent.*

There's also tons of beautiful stuff about his family. This may be what astonishes me most, given that Bobby was in late adolescence, a time when most kids morph into ruthless family vivisectionists. Yet he devotes page after page to how much he loves and admires Helen, Bob Sr., and Jeff. In May 1995, for instance, he wrote about discovering that Bob Sr.'s father had been an alcoholic. Bobby had had no inkling. *He made sure that he didn't give me the bullshit*, Bobby wrote of his own father.

> He made sure I had something better, and only asked that I do my best. That's all he asked. That's all my mom asked. And I want so badly to make them proud, even more proud than they already are. They deserve the pride. They deserve more than I can ever give them, and yet they will never ask for more than me. I love them so much.

You can hardly blame Helen for wanting to hear what he had to say once he'd become a young man.

JEN COBB, NOW MIDDLETON, wears her hair long, rather than in her old pixie cut, but her style and demeanor remain the same. She is still animated, still gracious, still beautiful to look at; when I walk up to her door in Washington, D.C., she greets me with a long hug. There are rescue dogs, there are sunlit rooms, there is a kitchen straight from a Nancy Meyers film. (I half-expect Meryl Streep to come gliding up with a tray of unbaked croissants.)

Jen has made for herself what is, to all outward appearances, a lovely life. But she had to assemble that life brick by brick, and she works hard to keep the joints from coming apart.

When I spoke briefly with Helen about Jen, she made an astute observation: Jen came from a family with lots of money but little love, while the McIlvaines had lots of love but little money. Jen says that yes, that's partly true, though her mother was a loving soul; she just didn't see enough of Jen's life. Susan E. Cobb died on April 20, 2001, less than five months before Bobby did, of a cancer that spread slowly, then fast.

Which is to say: On September 11, Jen was already a husk of herself.

Jen's father, her remaining parent, was highly successful but only narrowly rational, a bully and a screamer. This had predictable consequences in her romantic life: Jen always demanded complete control. She was done being bossed around.

Then along came Bobby, asking for more vulnerability and a shared say in both of their lives. Somehow, she trusted him. They first met a couple of years earlier, at the PR firm Burson-Marsteller, and around the office, he was known as the good guy who made everyone feel important. The inveterate romantic, he made *her* feel important, asking question after question about her family, writing her love notes for no reason. For her 27th birthday, on December 6, 2000, he asked my brother to scram and rearranged the furniture in their apartment to turn it into a restaurant, where he cooked her a three-course meal.

Jen would later learn that the dinner was a dry run for a proposal. She put a hold on the Ritz-Carlton in Philadelphia for October 20, 2002.

When her mother died, Jen could barely function. Her mother was the one who'd protected her from her father's storms of rage; she was the one who'd chatted with her late at night after Jen had spent a boisterous evening out with girlfriends. Yet Bobby remained steadfastly by her side, making the intolerable seem survivable. He would be with her every step of the way. She would still be loved.

Then Bobby died. The world became a mean, untrustworthy place. "There was not one thing I could control," she says. "Not one thing at all."

JEN KEEPS A STEAMER TRUNK of Bobby's things in the attic above her garage. In anticipation of my arrival, she's brought his belongings down in a turquoise canvas bag. She starts sifting through it. "There's the diary," she says, pointing. "The thing that caused all that trouble."

Bobby's other two diaries were hundreds of pages long. This one, I will shortly discover, had only 17 pages of entries. All that fuss over what was barely a pamphlet.

Then again, they're a dense 17 pages.

Jen has no memory of getting the diary from Bob Sr. But she does remember reading it immediately, voraciously, and returning to it night after night. She remembers, too, Helen asking for it back, though the tensions didn't start immediately. At first, everything was fine. Helen even gave her the engagement ring Bobby had bought for her. It was awkward and unceremonious— "He'd have wanted you to have this"—but Jen was grateful, and she wore it everywhere for months.

At some point, though, Helen started getting more vocal about that diary. "In hindsight, I don't know what my problem was," Jen says. "I was probably in pain and

A

also grasping for control and wanted something of his that no one else had. It seems kind of ridiculous now. It's just how I felt at the time—that it was mine and I wanted it to be mine and I didn't want anyone else to have it. It probably felt like it was all I had left."

What I had to understand about those awful, leaden days, Jen says, is that she wasn't just depressed. She was wretched—"double grieving," as she puts it, for her mother and then her future husband. When her mother and Bobby died in rapid succession, she fell into a deep depression, though she did her valiant best to conceal it. She still has anxiety attacks to this day. "When something upsets me," she says, "it goes downhill fast."

Which all makes perfect sense, I say. The only thing I can't understand is why she refused to transcribe the nonpersonal parts of Bobby's diary for Helen. That's not the act of a depressed person or a grieving person. That's the act of someone who's angry. She must have been upset with Helen for some reason, no?

Here Jen pauses. Then she starts measuring her words. "This isn't a knock on Helen at all," she says. "I'm so beyond it. But at the time I remember resenting that she said, 'You're going to be okay, because you're young.'" Jen recognized that there was a difference between their two losses. "But it felt like she was saying my grief was less important than hers. I know it was coming from a place of extreme pain, but I remember thinking, *How does she know I'm going to be okay? What if I'm* not *okay? What if I have a different kind of not-okay?*"

One thing you don't say to a person who's mourning, Jen tells me, is that they're going to be okay. She might have added: Nor do you say that to a depressed person. Depression does that—convinces you that you are never going to be okay.

"Now I get it," she says. Because of course Helen was right. Jen did find love again. But at the time, she was convinced that she wouldn't. She considered freezing her eggs. Once, in a moment of near-hallucinatory panic, she wondered if she could get impregnated with Bobby's DNA from strands of hair he'd left in a comb.

"It just would've come out better if she'd said: 'This is really sucky for you. And I'm sorry. Chances are, you'll meet somebody.' I guess there was just a nicer way to say it," she says. "However she said it set me off. Just because of my own personal shit."

I ask if it's possible that Helen *did* say those things, though she may have said a few artless things too. Maybe Jen missed them—or heard insults that weren't necessarily intended as such—because she'd grown up in a house that required an extra set of threat detectors, given her father's volatility.

A

"A hundred percent," she says. "It was probably me regressing into a little, you know, tantruming child. I was mad at the world. Of course she didn't intend to hurt me. She's the nicest person."

She and Helen are more similar than either of them realizes. Like Helen, Jen believed, at the time, in hiding her grief. Like Helen, she today takes refuge in the idea that Bobby's soul is rattling about somewhere. "I'm really showing my woo-woo side here," she says, "but I think that he'll be back, and I'll be back, and we'll finish our unfinished business."

And like Helen, she has learned to let a lot of things go. That's one of the most ruthless lessons trauma teaches you: You are not in charge. All you can control is your reaction to whatever grenades the demented universe rolls in your path. Beginning with whether you get out of bed. "And that's where I started my day, literally," she says. For years.

Today, Jen is choosing to hand me Bobby's diary as I'm walking out the door and heading back to New York. She has zero reservations about it. She says she'd like to have the original copy back, but there's no rush; the McIlvaines are free to read all of it, free to make as many photocopies as they'd like.

"I would have done it years ago," she tells me. "I think about them all the time."

Before I leave, I ask if she remembers where the phrase *Life loves on* comes from. She looks at me blankly. "I don't even remember him *saying* that. Is it in a book that he liked or something?" Tried that, I say. Searched Google Books. Nope. "Or was it a hymn?" Hymns aren't my strong suit, but I don't think so. I tell her that the McIlvaines are certain Bobby wrote it somewhere, but never mind, this is not her problem. I'll keep looking.

A

Jen and Bobby in 2001.
(Danna Singer; original photo by Sarah Mason courtesy of Jen Middleton)

MEMORIES OF TRAUMATIC EXPERIENCES are a curious thing. Some are vivid; some are pale; pretty much all of them have been emended in some way, great or small. There seems to be no rhyme or reason to our curated reels. We remember the trivial and forget the exceptional. Our minds truly have minds of their own.

Jeff, for instance, remembers that Jen stayed at his parents' house for half a year after Bobby died, while Helen says it was one week, and Jen thinks it was probably two months.

Or here's another: Jen remembers that Jeff gallantly slept in Bobby's childhood bedroom while she stayed with them, so that she wouldn't have to be traumatized by waking up to all of Bobby's things, while Jeff remembers *her* sleeping in Bobby's bedroom, and bravely waking up each day to all of Bobby's things.

And strangest of all: Though no one can remember where *Life loves on* came from, everyone—and I do mean everyone (Jen, Jeff, Bob Sr., and Helen)—once knew.

It's from Jen's eulogy. Which she based on Bobby's diary. The one she kept for 20 years.

"This past week I have been searching for some sort of comfort to get me through the shock of losing the love of my life," she told the mourners at Queen of Peace Church. "I came across one of Bob's journals and as I opened it, I said to myself, 'Please let there be some-thing in here that will comfort me.'" Then she described finding this passage, which Bobby had written as her mother was dying. She read it aloud.

It is OK for people to die. It hurts, and it is a deep loss, but it is OK. Life loves on. Do not fear for those who are dying. Be kind to them. And care for them.

"Life loves on," she repeated to the crowd. "After I read this, I vowed that very instant to love on in my life, just as I had made a promise to my mom to never let her be forgotten. It was a way that I could extend a life cut short."

The only reason I know this is because my brother found a copy of Jen's eulogy. Jen had tossed hers out. She is not, as she says, a saver.

Somehow she'd completely forgotten those words, as well as their provenance. And the McIlvaines had for-gotten where they came from, too, even though Helen wears them in an engraved bracelet and Bob Sr. enshrined them on his skin.

Then I remembered what Helen told me about Jen: *She became a nonperson to me.* She kept the words. But not Jen. She buried her future daughter-in-law too that year, just as she did her son.

HELEN RECENTLY TOLD ME a story about a long week-end she'd spent with Jen, maybe 10 days before Bobby died. The whole family was vacationing in Cape May. She, Bobby, and Jen were sitting on the beach, staring at the waves, with Bobby in the middle. It was a moment of gentle bliss. Helen turned ever so slightly toward Bobby to run her hand through his hair. But at that exact same moment, that very second, Bobby turned to do the same to Jen.

It was then that Helen realized Bobby wasn't hers anymore. "I said to myself, *You gotta go take a walk and look at the real estate on the beach,*" she told me.

In Bobby's early diaries, the McIlvaine family may show up everywhere. But not in this diary. This diary is primarily about two things. And one of them is Jen.

> FEBRUARY 18, 2001: I love her, deeply. We communicate so well. We resolve splits between us so well. And all of this means a lot.

> APRIL 11, 2001: I miss Jen. "Big" part of my life, or descriptions of how much she means to me do not suffice.

> APRIL 22, 2001 [TWO DAYS AFTER JEN'S MOTHER DIED]: I am so sorry, Jen. So sorry for your hurt.

I know it is hard. I'll be here by your side—here to love you, to listen to you, to hold you when you need to cry.

It's no wonder Jen didn't want to part with this diary. Or that she read it every night.

Helen recognized this immediately. I sent her a couple of xeroxed copies after I returned to New York.

"The Jen piece was huge to me," she says, when we have a chance to talk. "I thought of this in the middle of the night: She loses this guy that she loves—and most importantly, who loves her. Now, where is the *proof* that he loves her? I mean, okay, the mother gives her the ring. That's good. But there are these wonderful words: *I love her, deeply.*" She marvels. "I never thought about that. Never. That she needed that, that validation."

She also recognizes what the diary is missing. "He didn't say, *I love my parents too.* He said, *I love her, deeply.*" Bobby was all grown up.

Helen now wonders about her own behavior in those awful months. She tried to show Jen affection. But she'd only had sons. She didn't *speak* daughter. And that reserve she was describing to me earlier, the reserve I didn't believe she had—it was very real. "What happens is, I have intentions sometimes and forget to say the words," she says. "She had to guess what was in my head."

At any rate, Helen is now clear on one very important point. "It would have been beyond Jen's ability, even if she was in a good mood, to say, 'Okay, here, I'm giving it back.' I really would have had to give her at least pieces of that, somehow. That wasn't for me to own. I really mean that."

For years, Jen had been painted as a villain for holding on to this diary. Yet there never would have been a dispute if she had already been Bobby's wife, or perhaps even his official fiancée. But Jen was suspended between worlds, without influence or status. "It must have felt horrible," Helen says.

The final entry in Bobby's diary is dated September 6, 2001. It fills the whole page. When I first read it, I was disoriented. Then I realized what it was. "I feel completely unprepared. Should I rehearse?" it begins.

> It should go something like this: Do you have a few minutes to talk? First, I'd like to say that it has been a pleasure—or maybe a great experience—or do I mention Jen first? Or, I have developed a very strong relationship with Jen, and along the way it has been great to spend time in Michigan . . . OR . . . yes—I've had the chance to grow close to Jen, and after a lot of very serious thought, and after talking to her too, I felt

that it is time to make a commitment to her. OR—after a good deal of serious thought . . . AND . . . out of respect for you as head of the family . . .

What I was reading was a script. Filled with fits and starts, but eventually he got there. Bobby was struggling to find the words to say to Jen's father, whom he'd see on September 9, to ask for her hand.

A

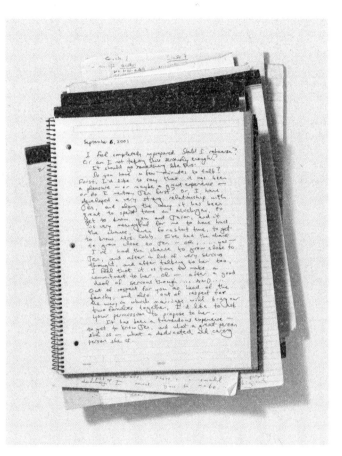

Bobby's final diary entry, a few days before 9/11. He was working out how to ask Jen's father for permission to marry her. (Jens Mortensen)

―――――

AT SOME POINT, not long after Jen gave me Bobby's diary, I sent a note to my editor, telling him that I had found, at long last, the elusive *Life loves on*. I took a photo of the passage and sent it to him.

Amazing, he texted.

But then, three pulsing dots in a bubble. He was still typing.

Except . . . I think it is (sort of) a misapprehension. Look how he writes his I's in other words. I think it says "Life **lives** on." But hard to say for sure . . .

It wasn't hard to say. He was right. I went through the whole diary again. On just the page before, Bobby had written, *I lived too long without thinking of "the markets" to suddenly care.* But it looks like "I *loved* too long . . ." His *I*'s look like backwards *J*'s, which can be mistaken for *O*'s, while his real *O*'s stand alone, like baby moons.

I texted Jen the same photograph I sent my editor. At first, she didn't see it. Then she did. Her initial reaction was the same as mine: anxiety, despair in the form of an expletive. Then:

Still makes me smile

Me: *What does?*

Jen: *That the people close to him saw and felt what they needed to. And that's ok. You know?*

I did. The phrase certainly sounded like something Bobby *could* have said. It was very Yoda, and Bobby was definitely very Yoda, spouting his little aphorisms about the drives of the human heart. To me, it was the difference between the spirit of the law and the letter of the law, or maybe what we do when we intensify the color of an image on our iPhone. We're not trying to create a fake; we're trying to align the image with the one that already lives in our memory.

We are always inventing and reinventing the dead.

You could make a case, weirdly, that Jen's withholding of the diary for all these years turned out to be a blessing. If she'd given it to Helen, it's possible Helen would have tucked it away in her safe for 10 years and barely read it, just as she did the other two diaries. Or maybe she'd have read it, but she wouldn't have *mis*read it.

Instead, Jen misread it, formed a eulogy around it, and handed the McIlvaine family an organizing motto for their grief for 20 years.

I still debated not telling the McIlvaines. I mean, the bracelet, the tattoo. But in a phone conversation with Helen soon after, I sensed an opening. I mentioned that I wasn't sure I was going to write about *Life loves on*. She

A

quickly intuited that something was amiss. "Because it was from somebody else?" she asked.

Kind of, I said. And I explained.

Helen was fine with it. She sees the unlikely beauty of this misunderstanding, even how it was a gift. But she holds out the possibility that the phrase still lurks somewhere. She remembers it as *Life* truly *loves on*, for one thing. And it's possible that I could have missed it in the hundreds of pages of Bobby's first two diaries. There are probably some missing diaries, too—why did he stop keeping them in 1995, only to resume in 2001?

So really, who's to say?

LIFE LIVES ON, LIFE LOVES ON—to me, it's irrelevant. There are far more beautiful observations in the recovered diary than that one, and they're prescient, eerie—much more germane to the McIlvaines' story once Bobby was gone.

Because the other thing his diary is about, the second thing, is grief.

In this way, the diary isn't just a time capsule. It's a crystal ball. Through an extraordinary twist of fate, Bobby spent his final few months thinking about what it meant to live with loss. He saw, through Jen's own mourning, that it could render you angry, irritable, skinless. He saw that grief could utterly consume. He wondered what the utility of all this sadness was, all this suffering. *Why do we have to hurt so badly?* he wrote. *Is that the way the person we lost would have wanted it to be?*

At one point, he guiltily wished that Jen would just make a choice to seize control of the things she could.

Yet somewhere amid all the passages of exasperation and dread—and many of them are quite detailed— Bobby comes to a much larger realization. It's an epiphany, I'm guessing, that made it possible for him to stick with his plan to ask Jen's father for permission to marry her, though he seriously questioned during those months whether she was ready. The date was August 20, 2001.

There are people that need me. And that, in itself, is life. There are people I do not know yet that need me. That is life.

To me, *that* is the most profound quote from the recovered diary. *That* is Bobby as Yoda. *That* is Bobby at his very finest, his most humane, his most mature. He understood that our commitments to one another are what we're here for—*and that, in itself, is life.* Even when those commitments are hard. Even when they cause us pain.

A

The ring Bobby had purchased in order to propose to Jen.
(Danna Singer; original photo courtesy of Jen Middleton)

ONE HESITATES TO SAY THIS. But if there was any path forward for the McIlvaine family, it was probably going to be through Jeff. Helen was careful never to burden him with expectations about marriage or kids—"You cannot put *anything* on the other child," she tells me— and he appreciated that. But it was thanks to Jeff, I think, that Bob Sr. and Helen started to muddle their way out of the dark. There were people they did not know yet who needed them. Among those people were their four grandbabies. The oldest one is named Bobby.

At 22, Jeff had a profound insight. "I remember thinking on that first day: *I can't let this ruin me.* 'Cause then what would Bobby think? Imagine if he knew that my parents and his brother were never able to recover. Imagine how bad that would make him feel."

He was reflexively answering the very question Bobby had asked as he watched Jen struggle with her grief: *Why do we have to hurt so badly? Is that the way the person we lost would have wanted it to be?* Jeff had a very clear answer: No. He had too much of his own life left to go. "I knew that if this ruined *my* life, *his* whole life was worthless," he says. "I wanted to work very hard to make sure that I had a good life."

It was so hard at first. "I remember I felt a responsibility to not die, which is a weird thing," he tells me. At the same time, he felt guilty for being the child who didn't die, thinking often of the dream sequence in *Stand by Me* when the father snarls "It should've been you" to his surviving son. He told no one at his first real job that his brother had died on September 11, because too many people were eager to share their own stupid stories about that day, always with happy endings. This delayed his ability to grieve for years.

But eventually, he built a rich, fulfilling life. He married a woman who could not only subdue his pain but enter an entire grieving ecosystem. He had four kids—four! two boys, two girls—and oh, the relief of not having to focus on himself!

I ask if he would have had that many kids if Bobby hadn't—

"No. I don't think I would have." Jeff lost his only sibling. He never wants any child of his to be in that position, should lightning ever restrike. "When you go through something like this," he says, "you realize that family—it's the *only* thing."

Those kids are now at the center of the McIlvaines' lives—even Bob Sr., who has chosen a path of daily suffering. As our conversation was winding down, he said something that stunned me: This 20th-anniversary year—a big one for the people in his world, filled with

TV interviews and conferences—may be his last of 9/11 activism.

I wasn't sure I believed it. I remain unsure. This has been his life for 20 years. Still: Maybe it's time for a change. "I'm sick of being angry," he told me. "That's the beauty of my life now. I can really separate. I truly can. To be out to lunch with Penelope . . ."

Penelope is his youngest granddaughter. He and Helen had lunch with her every Wednesday after pre-school before the pandemic. Jeff and his wife and children rely so heavily on Bob and Helen that they recently rented an apartment five minutes from Jeff's house, though they live less than an hour away.

Helen can't get over having little girls in her life. They have so many opinions! She still gets depressed sometimes. She'll have a beautiful moment, then realize that Bobby isn't here to share it. "But then it'll go away," she says. "I mean, being needed—not everybody gets four grandkids."

Yes. Being needed. That is everything.

BOBBY WOULD HAVE BEEN 46 this September. Jeff used to have vivid dreams about him, and man, how he loved them. They were brothers again, just talking, resuming their old rhythms and habits. But he seldom has those dreams anymore. "I haven't seen him in 20 years, you know?"

He says he almost wishes sometimes that he could trade his current well-being for the suffering he felt 20 years ago, because Bobby was so much easier to conjure back then, the sense-memories of him still within reach. "No matter how painful September 11 was," he explains, "I had just seen him on September 6."

It's the damnedest thing: The dead abandon you; then, with the passage of time, you abandon the dead.

It's really not surprising that Jeff should have this fantasy from time to time, to trade his happiness for just one chance to see Bobby again in a warmer hue. As Bobby wrote in that last diary, suffering, or the prospect of it, is the price we're willing to pay for the bonds we make.

Helen has found herself in the grip of a similar reverie. Recently, she was out with her limping group, and as she was looking around the table, staring in gratitude at these women who have held her up these past 20 years, a thought occurred to her. "I wondered, *What if God said, 'Okay, look, we gotta rewind here.' Would we go through all of this again?*"

Would they be willing to relive their same lives, give birth to those same children, fall in love with them and then lose them a second time? "And I know that every single one of them would have said, emphatically, yes."

A

For Helen, nothing in this world has rivaled the experience of raising her two boys. One of them, Robert George McIlvaine, died before his life truly began. But what would she have done without him, or he without her? For 26 years, she got to know this boy, to care for him, to love him. It was a privilege. It was a gift. It was a bittersweet sacrifice. *And that, in itself, is life.*

The McIlvaines on vacation in Cape May, New Jersey, in 2021.
Courtesy of the McIlvaine family.

ABOUT THE AUTHOR

JENNIFER SENIOR is a staff writer at *The Atlantic* and winner of the 2022 Pulitzer for Feature Writing for this essay, originally titled "Twenty Years Gone." Prior to joining *The Atlantic*, she spent five years at *The New York Times*—first as one of its three daily book critics, then as a columnist for the Opinion page. Before that, she spent eighteen years as a staff writer for *New York Magazine*, writing profiles and cover stories about politics, social science, and mental health. Her book, *All Joy and No Fun: The Paradox of Modern Parenthood*, spent eight weeks on *The New York Times* bestseller list; was named one of *Slate*'s Top 10 Books of 2014; and has been translated into twelve languages. Her work has been anthologized four times in *The Best American Political Writing*, and her profile of the psychologist Philip Brickman was selected for *The Best American Science Writing of 2021*. In addition to the Pulitzer, Senior has won a variety of journalism prizes, including a GLAAD award, two Front Page Awards from the Newswomen's Club of New York, a National Magazine Award (also for her story about the McIlvaines), and the Erikson Prize in Mental Health Media. She lives in New York with her husband and son.